ŠEVČÍK

VIOLIN STUDIES

OPUS 9

PREPARATORY STUDIES IN DOUBLE STOPPING

VORSTUDIEN FÜR DOPPELGRIFFE

ÉTUDES PRÉPARATOIRES POUR LES DOUBLES CORDES

BOSWORTH

BOE005164
ISBN: 1-84609-011-3
Music settting by Musonix

Editor: Millan Sachania

Cover design: Miranda Harvey
Cover picture: The Farmouth Stradivari, Cremona 1692 (Antonio Stradivari)
© Christie's Images Ltd.

Exclusive Distributors:
Hal Leonard
7777 West Bluemound Road
Milwaukee, WI 53213
Email: info@halleonard.com

Hal Leonard Europe Limited
42 Wigmore Street
Marylebone, London, W1U 2RN
Email: info@halleonardeurope.com

Hal Leonard Australia Pty. Ltd.
4 Lentara Court
Cheltenham, Victoria, 3192 Australia
Email: info@halleonard.com.au

Otakar Ševčík Opus 9

Sevčíks Vorstudien für Doppelgriffe legen seit mehr als einem Jahrhundert Tausenden von Violinisten ein sicheres Fundament. Sie behandeln nicht nur alle grundlegenden Doppelgriffe, sondern helfen auch, eine ausgeglichene und entspannte Haltung der linken Hand zu entwickeln.

Die Übungen sind hocheffektiv, wenn man sie ganz ohne Vorzeichen ausführt wie in diesem Band dargestellt, doch wenn man sie nachfolgend in anderen Tonarten spielt, sind sie noch wirksamer.

Die Finger zusammen setzen.

In den Übungen 3, 5, 7 und 16 werden die beiden Töne des Doppelgriffs zunächst einzeln und dann zusammen gespielt. Am Anfang setzt man die Finger eben gerne einzeln, einen nach dem anderen; doch sollen Sie so bald wie möglich die Gewohnheit entwickeln, beide Finger gleichzeitig auf die Saite zu setzen.

Das Zurückgreifen vom oberen Finger.

Für die meisten Hände, ob groß oder klein, ist es vorteilhaft, die Hand auf den oberen Fingern des Doppelgriffs zu balancieren, d.h. auf dem dritten oder vierten Finger - wobei die unteren Finger das Gefühl haben zurückzugreifen, und nicht auf den unteren Fingern zu balancieren und die oberen Finger vorzustrecken.

Beginnen Sie beim Ausführen der Terzen in Übung 14 damit, die Hand für den dritten Finger zu positionieren, so dass dieser gekrümmt, entspannt und bequem liegt. Achten Sie beim Zurückgreifen mit dem ersten Finger darauf, die Form und Lage des dritten Fingers nicht oder nur so wenig wie möglich zu ändern. Stellen Sie im zweiten Takt sicher, dass das Gleichgewicht der Hand auf dem vierten Finger ruht, wobei der zweite Finger das Gefühl hat zurückzugreifen.

Eine Hilfe für das Aufrechthalten der Balance der Hand auf den oberen Fingern ist es, den dritten und vierten Finger eher aufrecht als zu schräg zu setzen.

Wenn die Doppelgriffe wie in Übung 5 so aufgetrennt werden, dass erst die unteren und dann die oberen Finger gegriffen werden, geben Sie besonders darauf acht, die Hand nicht zu sehr auf den unteren Fingern zu balancieren, sonst muss der obere Finger zu sehr abgestreckt werden.

Den Bogen auf zwei Saiten führen.

Die drei Hauptfaktoren der Tonerzeugung sind Bogengeschwindigkeit, Druck und der Abstand zwischen Bogen und Steg.

Beim Doppelgriffspiel sind Bogengeschwindigkeit und der Abstand zwischen Bogen und Steg notwendigerweise auf beiden Saiten gleich. Es bleibt der Druck. Eine der ersten Herausforderungen des Doppelgriffspiels ist es, das Bogengewicht richtig und gleichmäßig auf den beiden Saiten einzustellen und zu führen.

Da das Gewicht auf zwei Saiten verteilt wird, benötigen Doppelgriffe doppelt so viel Bogengewicht wie bei einer Saite. Beide Saiten benötigen nicht notwendigerweise den gleichen Druck. Weil jede der Saiten eine eigene Stärke, Spannung und ein eigenes Timbre hat, benötigt jede einzelne Saite einen eigenen Druck, um die gleiche Lautstärke zu erzeugen.

Die Doppelgriffe intonieren.

Die Frage, die regelmäßig bei der Intonation von Doppelgriffen auftaucht, ist, ob der „dritte Ton" rein sein soll oder ob er ignoriert werden kann. Der „dritte Ton" ist ein tiefer Ton, oft tiefer als das leere G, der sehr leise im Hintergrund mitschwingt. Man nennt ihn den „Differenzialton", da seine Höhe von der Differenz zwischen den Frequenzen der beiden Haupttöne bestimmt wird. Im ersten Beispiel ergeben die Töne e und cis zusammengespielt ein a als „dritten Ton".

Was die Intonation kompliziert macht, ist, dass die genaue Tonhöhe davon abhängt, ob auf einer höheren oder tieferen Saite intoniert wird.

Wenn der fixierte Ton der tiefere der beiden Töne ist, muss der obere tiefer genommen werden, damit der „dritte Ton" sauber ist. Wenn der fixierte Ton der obere der beiden Töne ist, muss der tiefere Ton höher genommen werden.

Angenommen, Sie intonieren das h des ersten Fingers auf der A-Saite zum leeren d. Wenn der „dritte Ton" sauber sein soll, muss das h ziemlich tief gespielt werden. Spielt man dann dasselbe h zusammen mit dem leeren e, klingt das sehr unsauber.

Intonieren Sie aber das h zum leeren e, so dass der „dritte Ton" sauber ist, muss das h ziemlich hoch genommen werden, und es klingt dann sehr unsauber zusammen mit dem leeren d.

Wenn man dieses h als einzelne Note und nicht als Teil eines Doppelgriffs mit einer leeren Saite spielt, ist ein Mittelposition zwischen beiden Extremen oft die beste Wahl. Das kann zu interessanten Intonationsproblemen führen, die dadurch verursacht werden, dass man den Abstand zwischen den Doppelgrifftönen entweder mit dem sauberen „dritten Ton" spielt oder den „dritten Ton" ignoriert und die Töne so intoniert, als seien sie einzeln.

Übung 3 beispielsweise beginnt mit zwei einzeln gespielten Noten und führt dann zum Doppelgriff mit denselben Tönen. Das e des ersten Fingers auf der D-Saite sollte zum leeren e stimmen, auch wenn dieses e dann zu hoch für den sauberen „dritten Ton" des folgenden g-e-Doppelgriffs ist.

Wenn das e jedoch von Beginn an sehr tief genommen wird, so dass der nachfolgende Doppelgriff einen sauberen „dritten Ton" hat, klingt das e des Anfangs allein genommen zu tief. Da man den Finger nicht von einem zum anderen e bewegen kann, muss der „dritte Ton" ignoriert werden.

Manchmal kann man einen Doppelgriff so intonieren, dass der „dritte Ton" sauber ist, aber oft ist es wichtiger, die vorgezeichnete Tonart zu beachten und die Töne so zu intonieren, als wären sie auf zwei Spieler verteilt.

Ließe man Übung 1 beispielsweise von zwei Spielern ausführen, würde der Spieler der unteren Stimme ein normales c als kleine Terz über dem a spielen. Dieser Spieler würde kein sehr hohes c nehmen wollen, nur weil der obere Spieler ein a hält.

In engen Quinten stimmen.
Man kann das Problem des „dritten Tons" teilweise lösen, indem man in „engen Quinten" intoniert, so wie ein Klavier (in „gleichschwebender" Stimmung) gestimmt ist und wie Streichquartette intonieren, damit die C-Saiten von Bratsche und Violoncello nicht zu tief sind.

SIMON FISCHER
London, 2004
Übersetzung: Bosworth

OTAKAR ŠEVČÍK OPUS 9

Ševčík's Preparatory Studies in Double Stopping have provided a secure foundation for thousands of violinists for more than a century. Not only do they cover all the basic double stops, but they also help to develop a well-balanced and relaxed position of the left hand.

The patterns are extremely effective when played without any sharps or flats, as presented throughout the volume, but if then played in other keys, they become even more so.

Putting fingers down together.

In Exercises 3, 5, 7 and 16, the two notes of the double stop are played on their own before being played together. In the beginning you may like to put your fingers down separately, one followed by the other; but as soon as possible form the habit of placing both fingers on the string simultaneously:

Reaching back from the upper finger.

Most hands, large or small, benefit from balancing the hand on the upper finger of the double stop, i.e., the third or fourth fingers — with a feeling of reaching back with the lower fingers — rather than balancing the hand on the lower fingers and stretching forward with the upper fingers.

In playing the thirds of Exercise 14, begin by positioning the hand to favour the third finger, so that it is curved, relaxed and comfortable. As you reach back with the first finger, do not change the shape or position of the third finger, or at least change it as little as possible. In the second bar make sure that the balance of the hand favours the fourth finger, with a feeling of reaching back with the second finger:

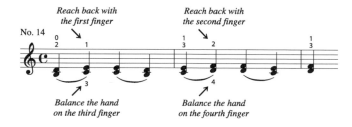

One way of helping to maintain the balance of the hand on the upper fingers is to make sure that you place the third and fourth fingers quite upright rather than too sloping.

When splitting the double stops, as in Exercise 5, so that you play first the lower finger and then the upper finger, take great care not to balance the hand too much on the lower finger, else you will have to stretch too much up to the upper finger:

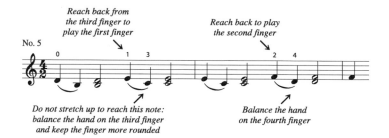

Balancing the bow on two strings.

The three principal factors in tone production are bow speed, pressure, and the distance of the bow from the bridge.

In playing double stops, the speed of the bow and the distance of the bow from the bridge are necessarily the same on both strings. The remaining factor is pressure. One of the first challenges in playing double stops is to balance and adjust the weight of the bow correctly and evenly on the two strings.

Because the weight is distributed between two strings, double stops may require twice the weight required by a single string. The two strings do not necessarily require equal pressure. Because each string has a different thickness, tension and timbre from the next, the individual strings may demand differing amounts of pressure in order to create equal volume.

Tuning the double stops.

The question that arises most frequently in tuning double stops is whether the 'third tone' should be in tune or whether it may be ignored. The 'third tone' is a low note, often lower than the open G, that drones very softly in the background. It is called the 'differential tone', since its pitch is determined by the difference between the frequencies of the two principal notes. The notes E and C# played together will produce a 'third tone' of A, as in the first example:

One factor that complicates tuning is that the exact pitch of a note depends on whether you tune it to a higher or a lower string.

If the fixed note is the lower of the two notes, the upper note has to be flattened in order to get the 'third tone' in tune. If the fixed note is the higher of the two notes, the lower note has to be sharpened.

Suppose you tune the first-finger B on the A string to the open D. If you want the 'third tone' to be in tune you have to play the B quite flat. If you then play the same B with the open E, it sounds very out of tune.

If instead you tune the B to the open E, so that the 'third tone' is in tune, the B will have to be quite sharp, and it then sounds very out of tune when played with the open D:

In playing that B as a single note, rather than as part of a double stop with either open string, a place midway between the two extremes is often the best choice. This can lead to some interesting tuning problems, caused by the difference between playing double stops with the 'third tone' in tune, and ignoring the 'third tone' and playing the pitches as if they were being played singly.

For example, Exercise 3 begins with two notes played individually, and then gives the same notes played as a double stop. The first-finger E on the D string should be in tune with the open E; yet this E is then far too sharp for the 'third tone' to be in tune in the following G-E double stop.

If, however, you begin by playing the E very flat, so that the ensuing double stop has an in-tune 'third tone', the initial E on its own will sound too flat. Since you cannot move the finger from one E to another, the 'third tone' must be ignored.

Sometimes you can tune a double stop so that the 'third tone' is in tune, but often it is more important to consider the prevailing key and to tune the notes as if they were divided between two players.

For example, if Exercise 1 were performed by two players, the player on the lower line would play a normal C as a minor third above A. That player would not wish to play a very sharp C in the second bar just because the upper player was holding an A.

Tuning in narrow fifths.

You can partly solve this problem of the 'third tone' by tuning in 'narrow fifths', which is how a piano is tuned ('equal-tempered' tuning) and how string quartets tune in order to prevent the C string on the viola and cello from being too flat.

SIMON FISCHER
London, 2004

Otakar Ševčík Opus 9

Les Etudes préparatoires pour les doubles cordes de Ševčík ont fourni, depuis plus d'un siècle, une base d'apprentissage sûre à des milliers de violonistes. Ces études couvrent toutes les doubles cordes fondamentales tout en favorisant l'établissement d'une position équilibrée et détendue de la main gauche.

L'effet de leurs configurations, déjà très efficaces jouées sans dièses ni bémols, telles qu'elles sont présentées dans le recueil, augmente d'autant si on les joue dans d'autres tonalités.

Abaissement simultané des doigts.

Dans les exercices 3, 5, 7 et 16, les deux notes de la double corde sont jouées séparément avant d'être jouées ensemble. Au début, on peut abaisser les doigts l'un après l'autre, mais il faut dès que possible prendre l'habitude de placer les deux doigts simultanément sur les cordes.

Placement à partir du doigt supérieur.

Quelle que soit leur taille, presque toutes les mains se placent mieux en prenant appui sur le doigt supérieur de la double corde, à savoir le troisième ou le quatrième doigt, et éprouvent ainsi plus de facilité à atteindre la position des doigts inférieurs qu'en prenant appui sur les doigts inférieurs et en étirant les doigts supérieurs.

Pour jouer les tierces de l'exercice 14, commencez par placer la main autour du troisième doigt afin que celui-ci soit recourbé, détendu et à l'aise. Lors du placement du premier doigt, ne changez ni la forme, ni la position du troisième doigt, ou le moins possible. Dans la deuxième mesure, assurez-vous que l'équilibre se fait sur le quatrième doigt tandis que le deuxième doigt atteint sa position.

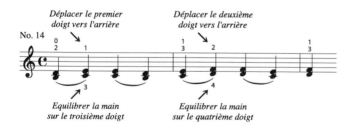

Assurez-vous de placer les troisième et quatrième doigt bien droits, en évitant de trop les incliner, de manière à maintenir l'équilibre de la main sur les doigts supérieurs.

Lors de la dissociation des doubles cordes, ainsi que dans l'exercice 5, en jouant d'abord le doigt inférieur puis le doigt supérieur, prenez grand soin de ne pas prendre un appui excessif sur le doigt inférieur qui vous obligerait à étirer trop fortement la main vers le doigt supérieur.

Equilibre de l'archet sur deux cordes.

Les trois composantes principales de la production du son sont constituées par la rapidité de l'archet, la pression de l'archet et la distance séparant l'archet du chevalet.

Lors de l'exécution des doubles cordes, la rapidité de l'archet et la distance séparant l'archet du chevalet sont nécessairement les mêmes sur les deux cordes. Pour ce qui concerne la pression, le juste équilibre impliquant la distribution correcte du poids de l'archet sur les deux cordes constitue l'une des principales préoccupations suscitées par leur pratique.

Le poids de l'archet étant réparti sur deux cordes, l'exécution des doubles cordes peut exiger une pression deux fois plus grande que celle des cordes simples, les deux cordes ne demandant pas nécessairement une pression égale. En effet, les différences d'épaisseur, de tension et de timbre existant d'une corde à l'autre, peuvent déterminer une force de pression particulière à chacune d'elles pour l'obtention d'un volume égal.

Accord des doubles cordes.

Le point soulevé le plus fréquemment par l'accord des doubles cordes est celui de savoir s'il faut aussi accorder le 'troisième son' ou l'ignorer. Le 'troisième son' est une note grave, souvent plus grave que la corde de *sol*, qui bourdonne doucement à l'arrière-plan. On l'appelle 'son différentiel' car sa hauteur est déterminée par la différence entre les fréquences produites par les deux notes principales. Les notes *mi* et *do* dièse jouées ensemble produiront le 'troisième son' *la*, comme dans ce premier exemple:

L'un des facteurs compliquant l'accord se situe dans le fait que la hauteur exacte d'une note dépend de son accord par rapport à une corde grave ou aiguë.

Dans le cas où la note fixe est la plus grave des deux, la note supérieure devra être abaissée de manière à ce que le 'troisième son' sonne juste. Si la note fixe est la plus aiguë des deux notes, la note la plus grave devra être haussée.

Supposons que vous accordiez le *si* du premier doigt sur la corde de *la* avec le *ré* de la corde à vide. Si l'on désire que le 'troisième son' sonne juste, il faudra jouer le *si* très abaissé. Si maintenant on joue ce même *si* avec le *mi* de la corde à vide, l'ensemble sonnera faux.

Si au contraire vous accordez le *si* avec le *mi* de la corde à vide de manière à ce que le 'troisième son' soit juste, le *si* devra être très haut et sonnera faux s'il est joué avec le *ré* de la corde à vide:

La meilleure solution pour jouer le *si* seul, et non associé à l'une des cordes à vide en double corde, est de l'accorder entre les deux extrêmes. Ceci peut cependant entraîner certaines intéressantes questions d'accord selon que l'on choisit de jouer les doubles cordes avec accord du 'troisième son' ou en ignorant ce dernier et en exécutant les notes comme si elles étaient jouées seules.

Par exemple, l'exercice 3 débute par deux notes jouées isolément, puis présente ces deux mêmes notes en double corde. Le *mi* du premier doigt sur la corde de *ré* devrait s'accorder avec le *mi* de la corde à vide. Toutefois, ce *mi* est alors trop haut pour que le 'troisième son' s'accorde avec la double corde suivante *sol-mi*.

Cependant, si vous commencez en jouant le *mi* très bas, de façon à ce que le 'troisième son' de la double corde qui en découle soit juste, ce premier *mi* joué seul sonnera trop bas. Puisque l'on ne peut pas déplacer le doigt d'un *mi* à l'autre, on devra ignorer le 'troisième son'.

On peut parfois accorder la double corde de façon à ce que le 'troisième son' sonne juste, mais il est souvent plus important de considérer la tonalité principale et d'accorder les notes comme si elles étaient réparties entre deux violonistes.

Ainsi, par exemple, si l'exercice 1 était joué par deux instrumentistes, le violoniste jouant la ligne inférieure jouerait un *do* normal comme tierce mineure au dessus du *la*. Cet interprète ne souhaitera pas jouer un *do* accordé très haut dans la deuxième mesure pour la seule raison que la partie supérieure de violon tient un *la*.

Accord en quintes étroites.
On peut apporter une solution partielle au problème de l'accord du 'troisième son' par l'accord par quintes 'étroites', correspondant à l'accord des instruments à clavier ('tempérament égal'), qui est celui adopté par les quatuors à cordes de manières à empêcher à la corde de *do* de l'alto et du violoncelle d'être trop basse.

SIMON FISCHER
London, 2004
Traduction: Agnès Ausseur

Per più di un secolo gli Studi Preparatori sulla Doppie Corde hanno fornito il fondamento sicuro per migliaia di violinisti. Questi studi non solo vanno a coprire tutti gli esercizi basilari su tale soggetto, ma aiutano a sviluppare una posizione rilassata e ben equilibrata della mano sinistra.

Gli esercizi sono estremamente efficaci quando vengono suonati senza diesis o bemolle, come sono presentati in tutto il volume; diventando ancora più efficaci quando suonati in chiavi diverse.

Mettendo giù le dita insieme.

Per quanto riguarda gli esercizi 3, 5, 7 e 16, le due note della doppia corda vengono suonate prima individualmente e poi insieme. All'inizio può essere preferibile mettere giù le dita separatamente, uno dopo l'altro, ma appena possibile si consiglia ad abituarsi a mettere entrambe le dite sulla corda simultaneamente.

Stendere all'indietro il dito superiore.

La maggior parte delle mani, sia grandi che piccole, traggono vantaggio da una mano che sia bilanciata sul dito superiore della doppia corda, cioè il terzo o quarto dito — avendo così la sensazione di allungamento all'indietro delle dita inferiori — invece di tenere in equilibrio la mano con le dita inferiori e allungare in avanti le dita superiori.

Nel suonare le terze dell'esercizio n. 14, iniziare mettendo la mano in posizione tale da favorire il terzo dito, in modo che sia curvo, rilassato e agevole. Mentre si stende il primo dito, non si deve cambiare la forma o la posizione del terzo dito, o almeno la si cambi il meno possibile. Nella seconda battuta accertarsi che la mano abbia un equilibrio tale da poter favorire il quarto dito, avendo la sensazione di un allungamento all'indietro del secondo dito.

Un modo per agevolare il mantenimento dell'equilibrio della mano sulle dita superiori è assicurarsi che la posizione del terzo e quarto dito sia abbastanza verticale e non troppo inclinata.

Nel dividere le doppie corde, come nell'esercizio n. 5, in modo che si suoni prima col dito inferiore e poi col dito superiore, prestare molta attenzione a che la mano non si bilanci troppo sul dito inferiore, altrimenti si è costretti a stendere troppo verso il dito superiore.

Bilanciando l'arco su due corde.

I tre fattori principali nella resa della tonalità sono la velocità dell'arco, la pressione, e la distanza tra l'arco ed il ponticello.

Quando si suonano le doppie corde, la velocità dell'arco e la distanza tra arco e ponticello sono necessariamente le stesse su ambedue le corde. Il fattore residuo è la pressione. Una delle prime prove d'abilità nel suonare le doppie corde sta nel perfezionare ed equilibrare il peso dell'arco correttamente ed uniformemente sulle due corde.

Stante la distribuzione del peso tra le due corde, le doppie corde possono richiedere il doppio del peso richiesto da una sola corda. Le due corde non richiedono necessariamente la stessa pressione. Dato il fatto che ogni corda ha uno spessore, una tensione ed un timbro diverso da un'altra, la corde individuali possono richiedere diversi livelli di pressione onde creare lo stesso volume.

Accordare le doppie corde.

La domanda che sorge molto frequentemente nell'accordo delle doppie corde è se il 'terzo tono' dovrebbe essere accordato o se dovrebbe essere ignorato. Il 'terzo tono' è una nota bassa, spesso più bassa della corda vuota del *Sol* che si sente soffocemente in sottofondo. Viene chiamato il 'tono differenziale', perche l'intonazione viene determinata dalla differenza tra le frequenze delle due note principali. Le note *Mi* e *Do* diesis suonate insieme produrranno il 'terzo tono' del *La*, come nel primo esempio:

Un fattore che complica l'accordo è che l'esatta intonazione di una nota dipende dall'accordo scelto, cioè se sulla corda superiore o inferiore.

Se la nota fissa è la più bassa delle due, la nota superiore deve essere abbassata per poter avere il 'terzo tono' intonato. Se la nota fissa è la più alta delle due, la nota più bassa deve essere alzata.

Supponiamo che si accordi il primo dito *Si* sulla corda del *La* della corda vuota del *Re*. Se si vuole che il 'terzo tono' sia intonato bisogna suonare il *Si* abbastanza basso. Se poi si suona lo stesso *Si* sulla corda vuota del *Mi*, si ha un suono molto stonato.

Se invece si accorda il *Si* sulla corda vuota del *Mi*, in modo che il 'terzo tono' sia intonato, il *Si* dovrà essere abbastanza alto, per cui si sentirà molto stonato quando suonato con la corda vuota del *Re*.

Quando si suona il *Si* come nota singola, invece che parte delle doppie corde con entrambe corde vuote, spesso la migliore scelta è data dalla via di mezzo tra le due estremità. Questo può condurci ad interessanti problemi di accordo, causati dalla differenza tra il suono delle doppie corde con il 'terzo tono' intonato, oppure ignorando il terzo tono e suonare le intonazioni come se fossero suonate singolarmente.

Per esempio, l'esercizio n. 3 inizia con due note suonate individualmente, e poi si hanno le stesse note suonate come doppie corde. Il primo dito del *Mi* sulla corda del *Re* dovrebbe essere intonato con la corda vuota del *Mi*; invece questo *Mi* diventa troppo alto per permettere al 'terzo tono' l'intonazione nella seguente doppia corda del *Sol* e *Mi*.

Se, comunque, si inizia col suonare il *Mi* molto basso, in modo che la doppia corda seguente ha un 'terzo tono' intonato, il *Mi* iniziale da solo suonerà troppo basso. Non essendo possibile spostare il dito da un *Mi* all'altro, il 'terzo-tono' deve essere ignorato.

A volte è possibile accordare una doppia corda in modo da avere il 'terzo tono' accordato, ma spesso è più importante considerare la chiave principale e accordare le note colme se fossero divise tra due suonatori.

Per esempio, se l'esercizio n. 1 fosse suonato da due suonatori, il suonatore della riga inferiore suonerebbe un *Do* normale come terza minore sopra il *La*. Tale suonatore gradirebbe non suonare un *Do* molto alto nella seconda battuta soltanto perchè il suonatore della riga alta manteneva un *La*.

Accordare in quinte strette.
Si può risolvere in parte questo problema del 'terzo-tono' intonando in 'quinte strette', cioè nel modo che si accorda un pianoforte (intonazione equabile o temperate) e come si accordano i quartetti d'arco per prevenire che la corda del *Do* della viola e del violoncello siano troppo basse.

SIMON FISCHER
London, 2004
Traduzione: Anna Maggio

OPUS 9

PREPARATORY STUDIES
IN DOUBLE STOPPING

VORSTUDIEN FÜR
DOPPELGRIFFE

ÉTUDES PRÉPARATOIRES POUR
LES DOUBLES CORDES

Übungen in Doppelgriffen	**Double-stopping exercises**	**Exercices en doubles cordes**	**Esercizi di doppie corde**
Jedes Beispiel und jede Variante in den folgenden Tonarten üben:	Practise each example and each variant in the following keys:	Travaillez chaque exemple et chaque variante dans les tonalités suivantes:	Studiare ciascun esempio ed ogni variante nelle seguenti chiavi:

No. 1

Oktaven	**Octaves**	**Octaves**	**Ottave**

Varianten
Variants
Variantes
Varianti

| * In den Tonarten Des und Ges sind die ersten und letzten Takte des Beispiels ausgelassen. | * In the keys of D flat and G flat, omit the first and last bars of the example. | * Dans les tonalités de *ré* bémol et de *sol* bémol, on supprime la première et la dernière mesures de l'exemple. | * Nelle chiavi di *Re* bemolle e *Sol* bemolle, omettere la prima e l'ultima battuta dell'esempio. |

No. 2

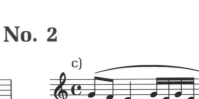

No. 3

Sexten	Sixths	Sixtes	Seste

2. Lage / 2nd position
2^e position / 2^a posizione

3. Lage / 3rd position
3^e position / 3^a posizione

No. 4

No. 5

| Terzen | | Thirds | | Tierces | | Terze |

No. 6

No. 7

Quarten | Fourths | Quartes | Quarte

etc.

No. 8

etc.

No. 9

Oktaven	**Octaves**	**Octaves**	**Ottave**
Nicht den 2. und 3. Finger anheben.	Do not raise the 2nd and 3rd fingers.	Ne soulevez ni le 2^e ni le 3^e doigts.	Non sollevare il 2° e il 3° dito.

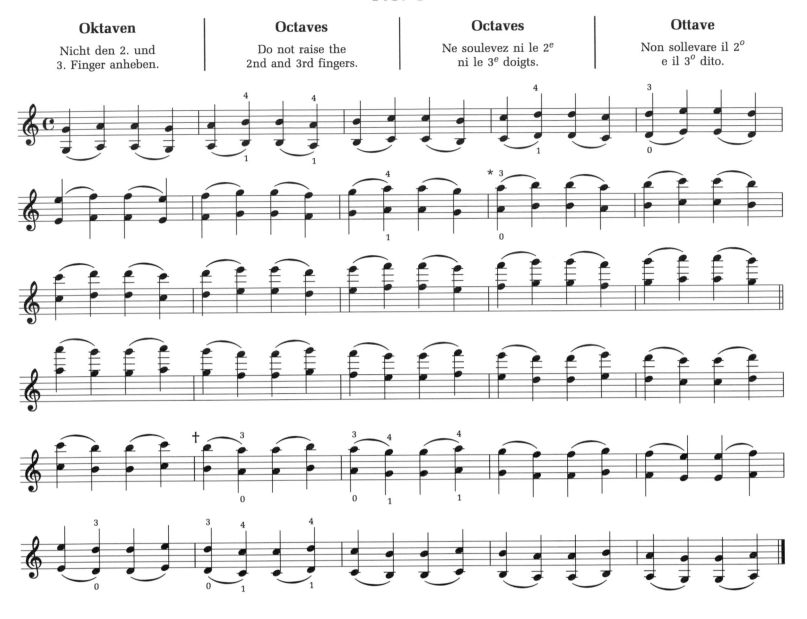

No. 10

etc.

No. 11

| Sexten | Sixths | Sixtes | Seste |

No. 12

No. 13

No. 14

| Terzen | Thirds | Tierces | Terze |

No. 15

No. 16

Sekunden | **Seconds** | **Secondes** | **Seconde**

No. 17

Quarten		Fourths		Quartes		Quarte

No. 18

No. 19

| Oktaven | | Octaves | | Octaves | | Ottave |

No. 20

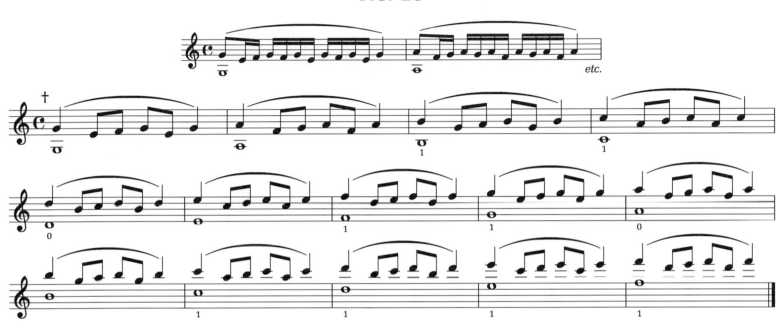

No. 21

| Sexten | | Sixths | | Sixtes | | Seste |

No. 22

No. 23

No. 24

| Terzen | | Thirds | | Tierces | | Terze |

etc.

No. 25

No. 26

Quarten		Fourths		Quartes		Quarte

No. 27

No. 28

| Duodezimen | Tenths | Dixièmes | Decime |

No. 29

No. 30

No. 31

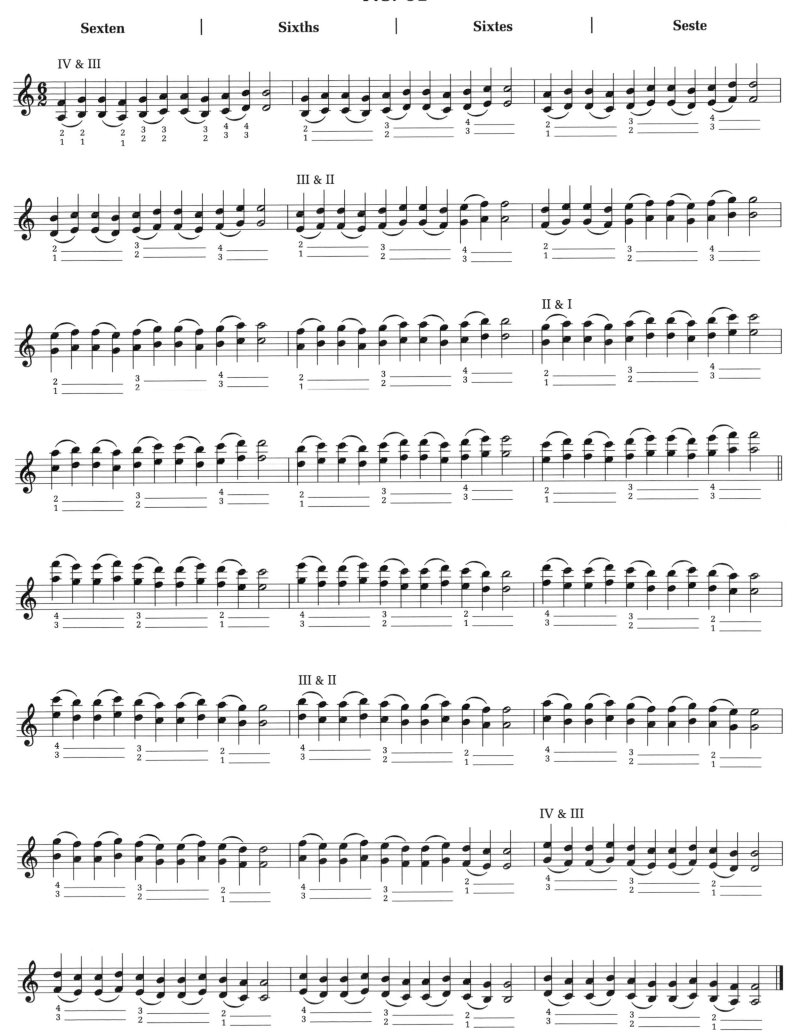

No. 32

No. 33

Terzen | **Thirds** | **Tierces** | **Terze**

No. 34

No. 35

No. 36

| Sekunden | | Seconds | | Secondes | | Seconde |

etc.

No. 37

No. 38

No. 39

Duodezimen | Tenths | Dixièmes | Decime

No. 40

Oktaven | Octaves | Octaves | Ottave

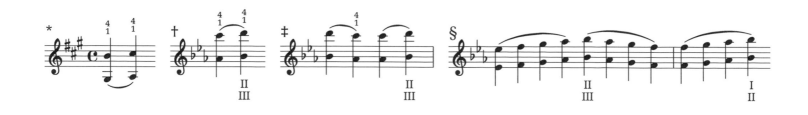

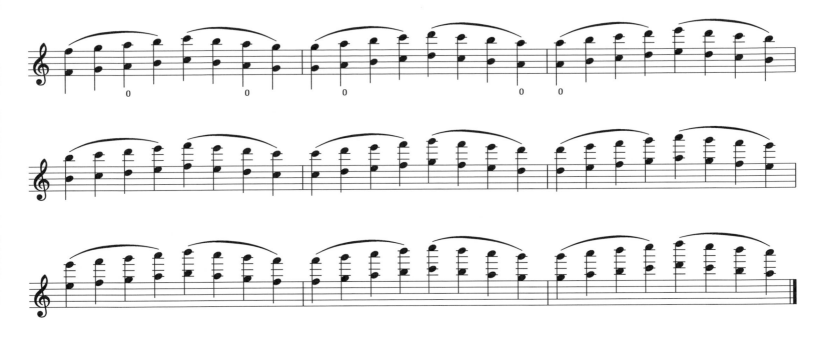

No. 41

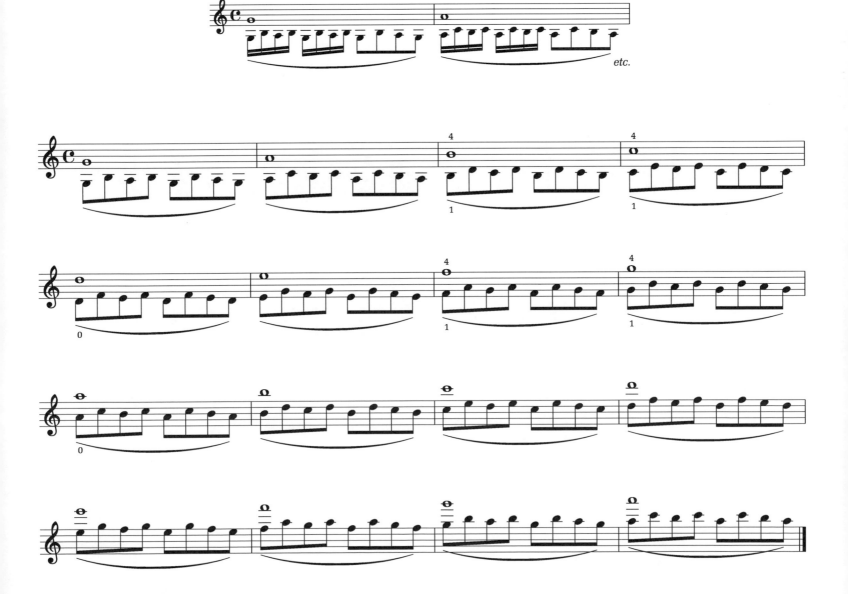

No. 42

Sexten | Sixths | Sixtes | Seste

No. 43

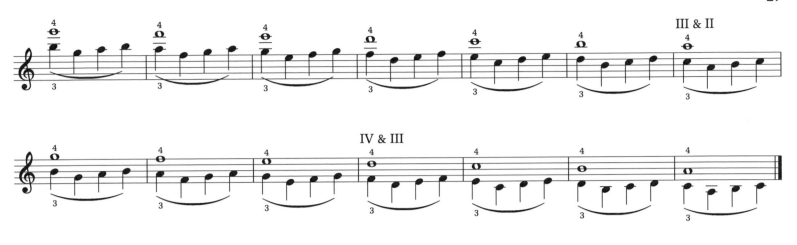

No. 44

Terzen | **Thirds** | **Tierces** | **Terze**

No. 45

etc.

No. 46

Quarten	Fourths	Quartes	Quarte

No. 47

No. 48

Duodezimen	Tenths	Dixièmes	Decime

No. 49

Sexten | **Sixths** | **Sixtes** | **Seste**

No. 50

Oktaven | **Octaves** | **Octaves** | **Ottave**

No. 51

Quarten		Fourths		Quartes		Quarte

No. 52

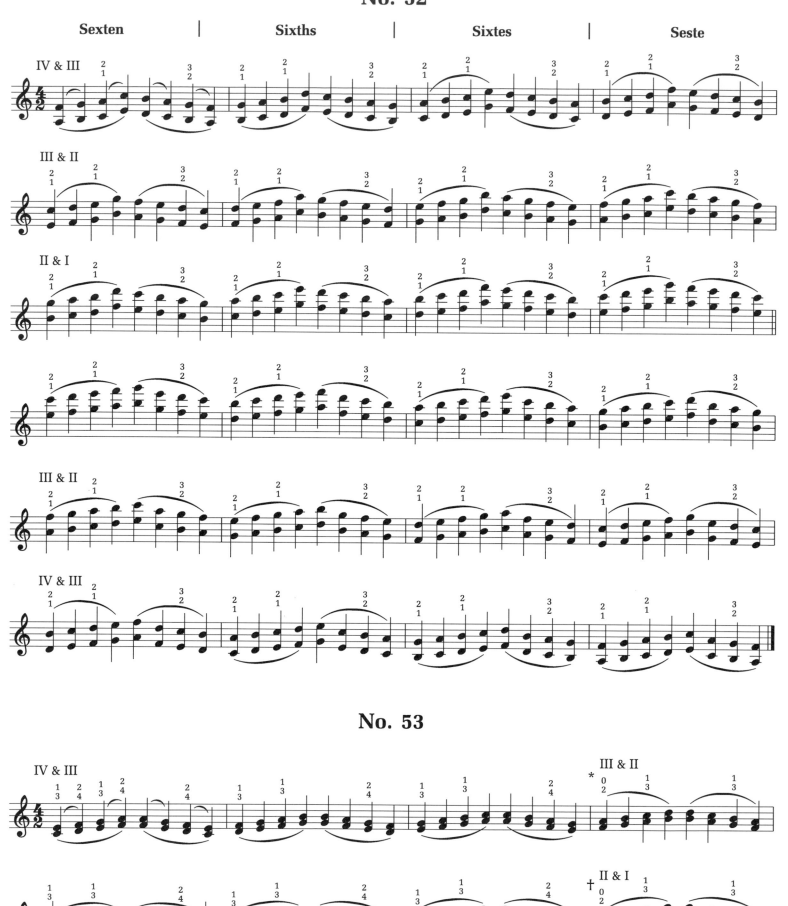

No. 53

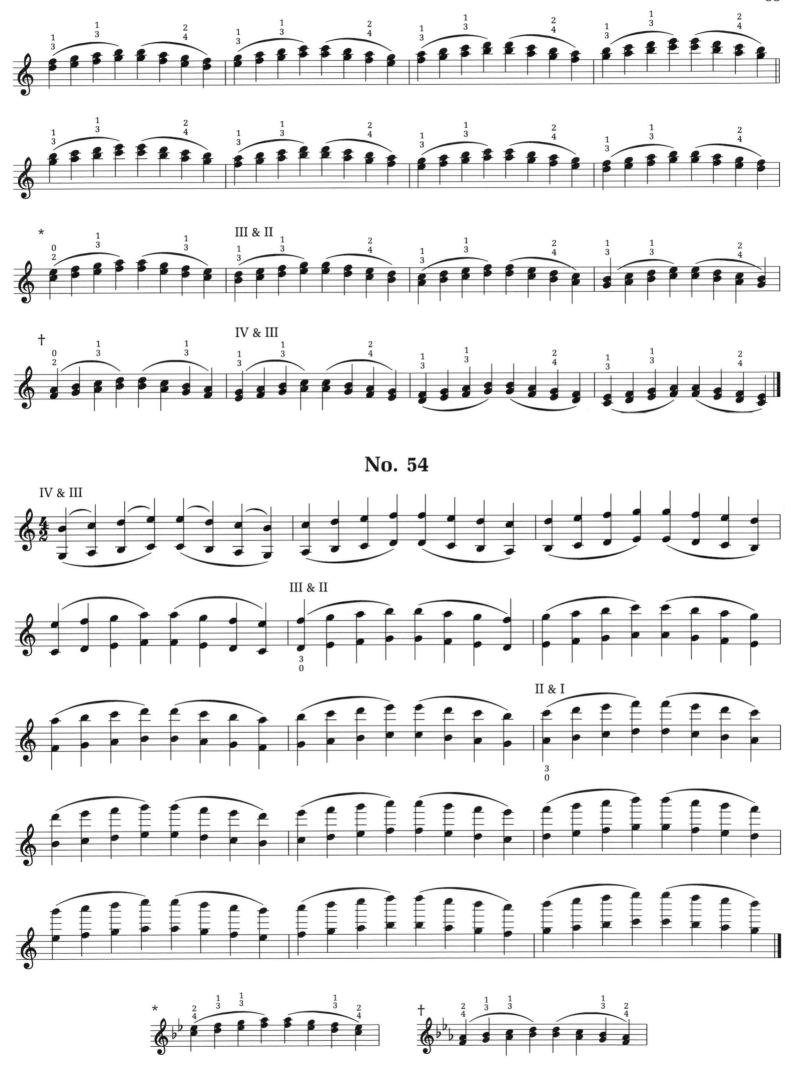

No. 54

No. 55

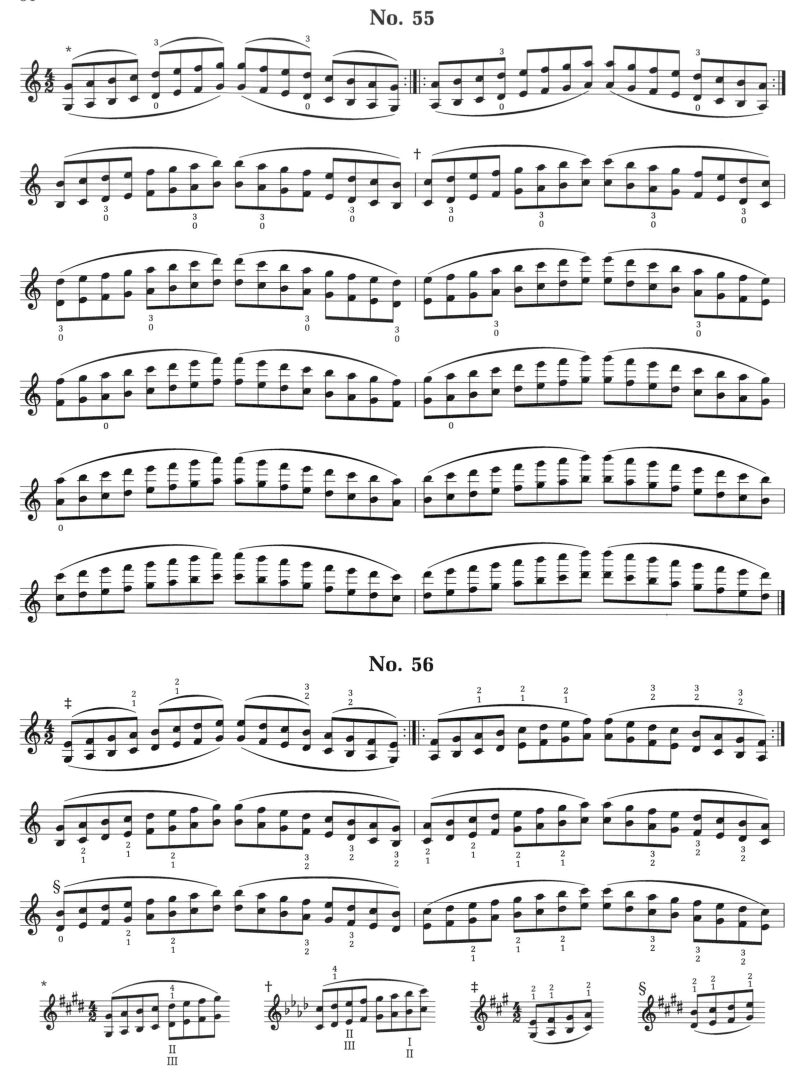

No. 56

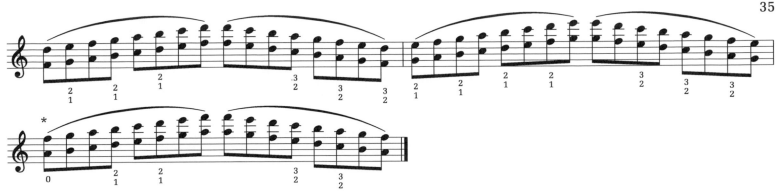

No. 57

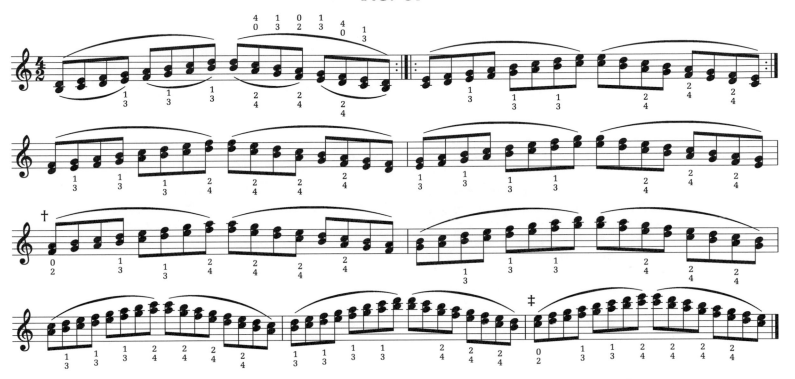

No. 58

| Flageolett | Harmonics | Harmoniques | Armoniche |

Typeset by Musonix